I0154355

Reassurance in Negative Space

REASSURANCE
in NEGATIVESPACE

POEMS BY

Elizabyth A. Hiscox

WORD GALAXY PRESS
An imprint of Able Muse Press

Copyright ©2017 by Elizabyth A. Hiscox
First published in 2017 by

Word Galaxy Press

www.wordgalaxy.com

All rights reserved. No part of this book may be used or reproduced in any manner whatsoever without written permission except in the case of brief quotations embedded in critical articles and reviews. Requests for permission should be addressed to the Word Galaxy Press editor at editor@ablemuse.com

Printed in the United States of America

Library of Congress Control Number: 2017930374

ISBN 978-1-927409-98-5 (paperback)
ISBN 978-1-927409-99-2 (digital)

Cover image: "Reflecting Space" by Alexander Pepple

Cover & book design by Alexander Pepple

Word Galaxy Press is an imprint of Able Muse Press—at
www.ablemusepress.com

Word Galaxy Press
467 Saratoga Avenue #602
San Jose, CA 95129

Acknowledgments

I am grateful to the editors of the following journals where many of the poems in this collection originally appeared, sometimes in earlier versions:

Aife: "Fourteen Minutes Too Late for the Cheese Counter" and "Reassurance in Negative Space"

The Ampersand Review: "Cakes and Ale"

Asylum Lake: "a call for catechresis," "Falling Off of One's Bedroom Slippers," and "Shrovetide and the Sugar Rush"

DMQ Review: "To Older Cold" and "Netsuke III: Snake"

A Dozen Nothing: "Cloud Vineyards," "Late Spring Travelogue, Outer Hebrides," "Phoenix," "A Poem with Three Lines from one Night in Portland," "Roles and Reckoning Near Solstice," and "Why Would Anyone Want to Live: Couplets for a Hero"

The Fiddlehead: "The Myrtle-Wood Bowl"

fromthefishouse.com: "*Cladonia rangifera,* Chernobyl," "The River's Mouth," and "Your body'd gone"

Gargoyle: "Vanguard Aria for Minor Organs"

Georgetown Review: "'Grand Rapids Arch'"

Gulf Coast: "The Pedestal"

Hayden's Ferry Review: "Reading Ostriker and *Archeology Today* for Spiritual Guidance," "Tallow, Candles and Light," "The Trapeze Is Always Flying," and "On Rereading a Line from *Leaving Resurrection*"

Ironhorse Review (Supplement: First Encounters with One's Own Femininity): "Preparing Trout Caviar in the First Trimester"

Matter: "Chival de Frise and Gone-Sweetness at the All-Inclusive"

Passages North: "The Red-Eye's Departure"

The Southeast Review: "Night Being the Consort of Chaos in Milton" [Gearhart Poetry Prize Winner selected by Erin Belieu], "Cellar Physic," and *"Or What You Will"*

Solo Novo: "The misnomer of Akira Kurosawa's *Dreams*" and "On Looking Again into Wright's *Forklift, Ohio*"

Watershed: "One argument for maple and pine-lined over marble"

Some of these poems previously appeared in the chapbook *Inventory from a One-Hour Room* (Finishing Line Press).

Foreword

There are moments of such attentive and exploratory linguistic resonance in this volume that the effect is alchemical: as we read along the lines, something changes in our awareness and becomes a new kind of *sound* insight. I am reminded of what Hank Lazer calls this aspect of the lyric, which activates and enacts a cognitive musicality: *thinking - singing*. Hiscox's poetry seems to me exemplary of this poetic element, for it is so often *thinking* via the *sound* of the words. Consider the closing couplet of a poem that begins simply as travelogue. "We are here," it opens matter-of-factly. Dazzlingly, eerily (the speaker having heard a lamb being butchered), we arrive at the following stunning conclusion:

> A shank an archipelago a fricative a plosive a butterfly a bone an
>   awareness of skill
> an acuity: the ease with which the air between us can be cleaved
>   and made knowable.
>   ("Late Spring Travelogue, Outer Hebrides")

The progress of the couplet seems to percolate through the bracing acoustic chain, but it leads to an exquisite—and excruciating—moment in which the Absolute is unexpectedly manifest. It's a sudden shift that bursts forth at the poem's end, but it's not singular. Hiscox arrives at such insight again and again as her poems pivot and dive. Another poem, contemplating the visual sparseness of abstract painting ("a lone line/ will indicate landscape"), makes a fine sonic connection, "there is tabula rasa to tableau." Beginning in pure *sound* similarity, the line tracks a Steinian arc of aesthetic praxis: the blank canvas becomes scenic because "one cannot not construct" ("a call for catachresis").

There is throughout this volume a deep and humane lyric wisdom, an almost fatalistically brilliant humor, perhaps culled from the loss of which Hiscox writes so wrenchingly in the central series of poems, which is at once elegiac and documentary of her mother's fatal illness. One of the major poems in this sequence, "The Pedastal," juxtaposes the clinical language of medical observation and the daughter's account of her mother's courage and suffering: "*Patient born at White Sands, New Mexico*"/ . . ."The mind is working, skin is trying-on slow sores." Such poems record the invisible consequences of a specific political history (civilians as the collateral damage of the race for the atomic bomb). The poems surprise us with piquant diction—"Glorious sparked synapses" of awareness; "aural nettles" of perception, "gleamtooth" of psychically integrated grief (one daughter, no two, lose one generation, no two, of women in the family).

Hiscox trains a laser eye on death, loss, and grief and does not flinch, but she will also be down to earth enough to find religiosity in a bowl of *soup*. Coincident with her intellectual verve is her sharp, wry wit. Thinking of Keats, she exclaims, "*Beauty is a blind alley.// It's the Truth. And this is why I can't ever/ get to what's next*" ("*Cakes and Ale*"). Think about the rare truth of that! Hiscox holds opposites in tension—philosophical depth and sparkling whimsy—and at the same time, she nimbly explores how far she can stretch the lyric (very far). The sheer formal range of these poems is marvelous, yet the volume retains an eloquent, tensile coherence of vision. These poems pulse with a complex and delicate insightfulness that neither dismisses sorrow nor submits to it. Here is a debut collection bold enough to cast an eye on Truth in poems that are both narrative (*storied*) and innovative, necessary poetry.

—Cynthia Hogue

Contents

vi Acknowledgments

ix Foreword

———

3 Tallow Candles and Light

5 Netsuke I: Crab

6 Reading Ostriker and *Archeology Today* for Spiritual Guidance

7 The Trapeze is Always Flying

8 Shrovetide and the Sugar Rush

9 The misnomer of Akira Kurosawa's *Dreams*

10 Inventory from a One-Hour Room

11 a call for catachresis

12 Or What You Will

14 Falling Off of One's Bedroom Slippers

15 Cellar Physic

16 Late Spring Travelogue, Outer Hebrides

19   On Looking Again into Wright's *Forklift, Ohio*

20   *Cladonia rangifera*, Chernobyl

22   Netsuke IV: Ashinaga & Tenaga

23   Sonnet to Room 411b

24   The Pedestal

26   Cakes and Ale

27   The Religiosity of Soup

29   The Red-Eye's Departure

31   On Rereading a Line from *Leaving Resurrection*

32   Preparing Trout Caviar in the First Trimester

33   Your body'd gone

35   The River's Mouth

38   Mead Memo Notebook Spiral, Yellow (II)

39   The Yield

43   Four for a Grandmother and Her Past

45   Netsuke V: Octopus

46   One argument for maple and pine-lined over marble

47   The Fourth Dynasty in Limestone

48   First Season's Monsoon

49   Cheval de Frise and Gone-Sweetness at the All-Inclusive

50   Cloud Vineyards

51   Phoenix

52   Early Artichokes

53 Tasting Notes for Two Liquid (de)Vices

54 Netsuke III: Snake

55 Shiny Magazine on the Finer Things

57 Fourteen Minutes Too Late for the Cheese Counter

58 Roles and Reckoning near Solstice

———

63 "Grand Rapids Arch"

65 The Complex of the Yolk Base

67 Netsuke II: [   ]

68 To Older Cold

69 The Myrtle-Wood Bowl

70 Why Would Anyone Want to Live (Couplets for a Hero)

71 Barcelona

72 Vanguard Aria for Minor Organs

73 Reassurance in Negative Space

75 A Poem with Three Lines from One Night in Portland

76 Night Being the Consort of Chaos in Milton

———

81 Notes

———

Deity is in the details & we are details among other details & we long to be
Teased out of ourselves. And become all of them.
　　— Larry Levis

The heart wants to be—
anything in it.
　　— Beckian Fritz Goldberg

Reassurance in Negative Space

—

Tallow Candles and Light

It is the story. That poverty
leads to consumption of light itself.

It is the sidebar that is, mysteriously, often the core.
It is the tallow candles after

six weeks' rain and longer fallow potato fields
that give warmth to systems entirely internal.

The trivial is not trivial. It is intimacy.
The rendering of fat, the rendering

down to a moment in the dark
where you take your hand,

take what's left of last fall's slaughter,
last November's open barrels,

that hot day of dipped wicks and swirl,
and unfold all in your palm like a sacrament:

keep this house alive for a number of hours.
Hours counted, *God willing,* on two hands.

Tsunamis, earth-shatterings, Minoan hair twist
of newly set curls cinched quickly under

tide and rubble—these are sex in the middle
of the kitchen floor. Sex in the town square.

I am speaking of corners. I am speaking
of the mirror held to nostril.

Netsuke I: Crab

You are the one I scuttle to first,
because I've taken you apart.
I know the joints of your legs,
that slight shell mocking the nautilus
with its gymnastics—you are not even
molehill in your ascent.

How can I want to hold you more
having consumed you, parsed you
out of being into mine.

Reading Ostriker and *Archeology Today* for Spiritual Guidance

And, what if we are just as much as the symbols suggest?
Peace and harmony; scissors on the table;
crystal skulls? Held to the light what wouldn't our minds
clip to bits, prism into shades of citrus fruit and strawberry,
try to parse into reconciliatory sound?

Damn the fathers. We are talking about defiance,
you say. I wonder. Like we haven't read tarot cards
at high altitude base camps—reviewed our plans.
Found absolutely everything wanting. Found absolutes.
Like chances aren't already the fiction of our peculiar taking.

All day I'm seeing fractions where none exist. Parallels
would be nice. I thumb an article on Lake Baikal's one-off species count,
that lake the "Blue Eye of Siberia."
The whole earth a head made of glass and that window to the soul
populated—are we surprised?—by the endemic. Native to our scope.

And what if our scope is only to focus? And, what if we are
as much as the symbols suggest? *The weddings of innocence*
and glory, innocence and glory. The gun on the wall in the first act,
I swear, could never make a sound—would still bear beautiful weight.

The Trapeze is Always Flying

Calls himself an artist, but he's just tide-riding
like the shag carpet catching light
on the night boat moored,
all disco and barbecue downwind—
downstream—from the cathedral.

In the over-etching of the bohemia glass
(that stained window for the lips' pressure)
a frog is dancing (ballet, hoop) and crickets bicycle.
Liqueur becomes sacrament to whimsy.

This is the renegade nature of tradition:
fraying at the edges of a century.
Generations eating their own eyeballs,

the flyer for a hog of unusual size
is a hundred-year-on legible
the gathering place is again
nasturtiums and lollipop wrappers:
no net and, as always, Free Admission.

Shrovetide and the Sugar Rush

Hearing *Gloria* again and again: en masse.
Amassed before yanked from Mass, the masses.

Mardi Gras, too, from every storefront, cracked car window:
Gonna make 'em all stand in place until I see the Zulu Queen.

Fatback and pancakes thick on the lips;
this is to make us remember what is lent:
a hairline moment of ecstasy and sound before
silence and ecstasy, *in excelsis Deo* day in, day out.

Doesn't seem like any way to approach a throne.
False kneel and pretense of an even keel.

Pass the chocolate rabbits, already. Hollowed joy.
Fertility and its absence run amuck.
All bright yellow and marshmallow.
Turn down the carnival of excessive absence.
Sluice me through to Sunday.

I'll be seeing you again, says the Zulu Queen. The King.

The misnomer of Akira Kurosawa's *Dreams*

is the Miłosz line I can't get right:
panting the boughs is not how the angels come.
This may be how Kurosawa went after
the inner sour: to imply the impure
exists within the confines of the holy.

All angels pant as surely as they part.
That under the apple trees
there's always going to be something stuck
in Adam's throat and one need not say.

Doesn't the very word nightmare frighten more
if implicit.

Inventory from a One-Hour Room

The universe: a bull of green slipped with purple
and dried daffodils in a pile on the lawn.
Moon dish rising,
armpits softening down the sides of hips,
you walk into the room in an apron with a candle snuffer.
Nativity calendar at the end of March, small doors still unopened and
a wooden bird with a low tail looking always west.
Tight-set hairstyle of a previous generation.
He sees the day and the cypresses and the marble
and a now child pulls a clutch of wild eggs from Easter's inside pasture.
"A bad neighborhood my sister in. Barred windows," she smirks,
and there's that low-slung bear-faced section of floor again.

a call for catachresis

a *wot not what* that painters know

when one discovers a horizontal line
a lone line
will indicate landscape

and a vertical will
to something quite different

the grin of a doorway
a loft of figure

any gesture   any color anatomizes

red rushing to
whoever views

there is tabula rasa to tableau   there is the first ~~impetuous~~° step

one cannot not construct

green always at a remove
any movement does
any line will do

° read "impenitent"

Or What You Will

Can we just acknowledge for a second that
most of us do wear jeans? Wear them often?
They are like a middle working class top hat—
future generations' jaws will drop and they'll say they all had them?
Those crazy black stovepipes. I thought it was just a thing,
but what a wonder and the feathers on the women's!
No wonder the birds went dead forever—went extinct, away.
Went is enough really but we want to twin words off.
It is funny not to have a twin.
It is funny not to have the same last name.
How do the Violas and Sebastians of this world do it, though?
Those political Clintons? How don't I?
My sister had the same name as me, but no more.
I don't say mine that way so there was never my mom,
who was also never like her mom
because she changed her name.
Which she? Exactly.
To have sisters and mothers and brothers
is not the same thing. To syntactically equate
an animal and humans is a misstep. All zeugma
and no respect. And it is also true because bears don't
carry the thorn of a last name in their left paw.

There's more reasons than that,
but that's exactly when
my own resilient dark enters and the existentialists
don't seem as off as usual. Don't hit me like Vespers at dawn.
In the novel I reread at these times
someone is at the opera and says
you have to choose.
There at Tristan and Isolde where everyone is choosing wrong onstage
and the narrator believes you have to choose.
Not how to die or what for—of love even,
I guess, if you want—but what to look at.
Who to watch who is watching who is choosing wrong.
The and . . . and . . . And some have opera glasses:
twinned lenses and polished brother, no, mother of pearl.
And by funny I mean look at everyone wearing jeans
and don't look away or you'll laugh—
thinking how easy it is to be in the world.
And someone who may be my twin will swallow
another sip of Madeira and order a pair of corduroys
from Amazon and not think about the river once because neither would I.
Would you. Wouldn't think of water at all. Of Noah. Of two-by.
Countless fish and eels and dolphins who don't come into it.

Falling Off of One's Bedroom Slippers

The glamor hammer of The Fifties is in full swing, as are the post-
world-war-two *what the bejeezus*
you can do that with your tongue? cocktail parties and the post-
world-war-two *what the*

bejeezus you can do that with your wife? complications alongside
acres of frozen food and cars that
couldn't stop on a dime if every toddler in the newly fashioned
suburbs were to toddle out

into my cherry-red pogo stick lollipopped jacks and soda hopped
version of The Fifties.
My grandmother is the one telling me the story and how it all ends
fairly badly with a split wrist,

a bone snapped, a woman collapsed out of her sex-me-up house
shoes down her single family
nightmare of a staircase with wall-to-wall: a place for everything
and everything in its Max

Factor and it's really no wonder that their daughters, my mother,
thought the only way to get rid of a
slip-on heel that was ready for meatloaf, mashed potatoes, and
from-behind was to burn it.

Cellar Physic

I.

Bull in a china shop: collecting the sound of Ming,
tumbling through Yuong and Song. Timpani
noise: sweet kettle thrum. Skin. The finality of the first
twitch. Dynastic shards crippling the polished floor
with clatter. An animal rotating in heavy light,
closed quarters, a cadence of hooves keeping time
with widening eyes, nostrils, rotations of neck,
gyres, motion made bright in its inevitable ephemeral.

II.

Pristine variation on the theme of sugar beet.
Liquid crystal endowed with cheek-flush, with undoing.
Vodka tune played out in orderly rows of breakable
engagements. Wild nights she'd called them.

III.

Anyone watching this woman alone in the rows
—her touching of the gilded lips, enameled feet—
sees her want to unleash her spine,
that flesh-hoop to the drumhead of her outer,
despite the causality of aisle. Like a lover, like one loved
bodily with overlay, intricacy of line, to be both
horn and hoof, and glaze. All pottery was wet once.
Held, but also thrown. What generosity the bull brings.

Late Spring Travelogue, Outer Hebrides

We are here. It's a smattering of tourist-encrusted rocks
    spun out onto the burred and tweedy sea.
Stornoway: all oceanic winds, mineral-tinged whisky,
    oats and battered fish, busting at the seams

with a vacancy of trees, an abundance of Neolithic light,
    the stones themselves standing in wait.
These dead isles twined, sold, silent, wrapped in white
    waxed paper, trimmed, and weighed.

Air burials by eagles, and we're chasing a dull purple
    sandpiper out Aignish Point to feel alive,
we wander in search of something that doesn't already
    know we are arrived.

Up-alley a chattering man is butchering a lamb in a
    language we don't understand but we
catch on to cadence: hands along, then within, a cavity
    and a thud clank dangle splice of tongue.

A shank an archipelago a fricative a plosive a butterfly a
    bone an awareness of skill
an acuity: the ease with which the air between us can be
    cleaved and made knowable.

—

On Looking Again into Wright's *Forklift, Ohio*

O! How the "o" in your typewritten script filled up with ink:
a sweet clot of visual sound.

Every such stroke stuck
and charred like lighting:

pinpoints of light become small shelters for darkness,
eclipses that mock back.

It is a wet spot of night that pulls one in and unleashes
soothes and *pool* into self-fulfilling.

IF LIFE IS A NEGATIVE
Then you are the darkroom.

Cladonia rangifera, Chernobyl

A dual organism:
low-slung show of "mutual."
reindeer moss, a misnomer—
a lichen: *tangled hollow stalks branching*
and rebranching. Stock slaughtered
for countries, for continents.

A young girl picking potatoes
brings her parents water.
Wind hurling branch, child, sound to the house,
then yellow earth after deep rain.

Sympathetic, the systems—
the ferns, heather, berries,
the forests—turn the sky inward:
spread the cloud in the fox's stomach;
Feed half-life again.

Wild mushrooms put to mouth:
a black broth and small busy hands.
Children put to rest after simple meals.

The chart on the schoolhouse wall:
rain to lake to fish to man.
Flake into the mouth, onto the tongue—
a rain to a gathering storm.

Fish, bellies round like the oversky,
feed the thick layers:
feed what has fallen out of the above
under the silver,
sliver knife.

There is a field of lichen
the wind cannot shift.

Netsuke IV: Ashinaga & Tenaga

Akimbo and bent like the straw slicked
over on itself,
you are Ashbery's Popeye's
Olive Oyl. Always depicted like
some rube. Yet are you not
also an implement of the gods? Made
by the gods: manipulate clod
of live ash (in ivory) in
their image?

Sonnet to Room 411b

A blue lung pulls its windpipe to the ground
so often that we are upping to cup the sky.

Hummingbird through the pane, sucking the Spanish roses
and my eyes are the girl passing me in the hall.

"Mother." It makes your mouth call
in the saying.

The ceiling fan becomes a turnstile for the anxious air
and a well-intentioned bedside: crepe-paper flowers fading to
fading, too.

Before I lay me down to sleep I pray the Lord.

The sternum starts neighing
and insomnia brings white cats to my lap.

A standard form with its sad slash of White Out and NEXT OF KIN:
Start embroidering your pain on the back of my neck.

The Pedestal

In hindsight this could be when it started
Stumbling: smile. Embarrassed late October jog.

Patient has no family history of this kind of problem
She is a rebel in this illness business.

MRIs done in '96 and '97 and the doctors found no lesions did not think
Remember? Whirl of light there just beyond your face.

Bowels are also wrapped in muscle that can become weak
A shitting-yourself, shitting-others future.

Some relief can be achieved with tilting of the chair or bed
The mind is working, skin is trying-on slow sores.

The purpose of the transfer board is to take the weight off the caregivers
The heart's real purpose: pump the weight of life. Of

A therapist must come to the home for an appropriate assessment
A stranger walks past nodding Iris planted deep:
those purple blooms, from Kim's third birthday, underfoot.
A stranger walks where you have kneeled and felt the earth.

This ankle is more frozen than the other side
That ice that took the legs is sheltering still, here.

One could be pushed into low levels of oxygen in the blood
Already one's been pushed past all of it, come back.

Some is genetics, some isn't, some is genetic predisposition
So there is daughter one. There's two. Say promise, time.

Patient born at White Sands, New Mexico
They said to finish families up before arrival.
On base, in that New Mexico you cried your birth.

Is this your daughter? It's good in times like these to have had kids.
This eggshell-puncture sickness thickens blood to blood.

Cakes and Ale

What list of India, what rite of spring can save me
from my simple adoration for the uncracked cup,
uncomplicated fan of wild rose, the way
a man can stand with moonlight full on his face?

What I believe—to the point of distraction—
is what you articulate so off-the-cuff
(at Keats's expense). It quakes, a promise:
Beauty is a blind alley.

It's the Truth. And this is why I can't ever
get to what's next. Switch-backing to catch again
a glimpse of globe mallow in the setting sun,
of radiance off Snyder's page. Corn kernel.

The Religiosity of Soup

My soup dreams of Palestine and, tangentially, Rio de Janeiro's giant
    Christo.
Of things clutched in translation to mouth. Like Chinese cum
    California hot sauce.

Of sriracha, which the best-parts-of are chili, sugar, salt, garlic, cobalt.
Actually, the opposite of that last, in color, which is one of the best
    parts:

the looking at it of it. Some things are right out there. Nobody
    bothers
to say. Like the other set of ears when a kid wears the bunny ears.

Jerusalem artichokes are misnamed twice, says David Attenborough.
"Twice," says he. And me, I think, *like the New World its damned self.*

Wheat thatched in neoclassical posters looks like hash browns
fixed on the head of the muse. It is ears too. But not.

The potato is the confusion there though you might say different.
Like eggs not over easy but side up, the not-chokes followed the sun,
    girasole,

yolk-love and the names they got, one of the things that's the
   most part of them:
that constant looking to heavens. The British come here: "Name
   it like a place we've heard of!"

And we weren't allowed off the cruise ship on Easter, not into
   Israel, but back out
into that sea, the one my soup knows, its crossings, the one that
   Christo stares back out at.

There's a living thing that turns to watch the signals the sky
   sends, sets down roots
only to have a mouth come and say choke scream choke and fight
   tooth and nail choke.

These new old wrong names, but it is not the opposite of. Just
   the flip. I'd tell David, "No.
No, they were dead on." Those sunflowers. They won't ever let
   you out of that sea on Easter.

The Red-Eye's Departure

In their sights like a Roosevelt Elk in stocking feet, they have me:
make antlers and count to nine. At the B Gates' screening
we herd and raise our hands behind our heads. Some look ready to
    recline
back upon imaginary pillows. Muscle memory, perhaps.

In one hour, in thousands of miles of air, the man on the aisle will be
in a Renaissance collar of sharply rising snores
falling only, like crisp lace, to just below the ear before scratching at
    sound again.
He does not sleep like you.

Aping a whirligig I saw in Provincetown—
the woman at my right dips down
for lavender pills, then white, and a novel remaindered and divested
    of its cover, bobs down again
for something for her lips, "so dry this high, thin air," and something
    for her tongue,

"cinnamon—would you?"—a whirligig, faux French, on a front lawn.
    A playful cancan of paint,
of plywood à la Moulin Rouge and a lean in to kiss and then kick and
    kiss and kick
when the wind was right.
And he does not smell like you. All Old Spice or cardamom.

I cry when I find Grieg tugging on the other end of the disposable
    headphones
for which I've paid five dollars to drown in sound to the other side of
    the country,
in the sandwich seat trying not to touch. Or be.
Trying to let go the image of that parade of people self-cuckolding for
    the homeland camera.

On Rereading a Line from *Leaving Resurrection*

I felt the hoarse break in his indrawn breath and then the long letting go.
—Eva Saulitus

In turn I, too, feel the break—
horse bolting toward *away*
across an open, oft-named field,
away in the sigh of any bereaved.

The form, at first, just out of reach:
wild-carrot close. Then gait
becoming light reflected
off the body of going. A silhouette

of tightness in the chest. Expectation
after the lengths of flower, song, Friday
mornings, late nights at the office,
in the ward—the bolt toward.

This is the long letting.
The LOST posters glued on every
telephone pole, every facet of your face.
The picture in the frame on the piano.

But I, too, am here—also bearer
of this burden. I draw it
not like line, or bow—straight as horizons of art or fact—
I draw it with you. This necessary shawl
called breath.

Preparing Trout Caviar in the First Trimester

The man who knows how is aided
by a woman who sees more. He admits.
He writes the book that I am scanning

on foraging, on making the most
of what life has given me to work with—
what life has been taken is what the woman

reminds the reader. She who is not color blind.
You see, he sees the skein of eggs and weighs
them "gray." She can see the red vessels,

that rope, the roe, the deep stain
that sucks its way into the cutting board
now braided with membrane and blood

and bright orange eggs. He can't see
beyond the orange. And calls the trout we caught
the "hen." What a haul at the henhouse

these hundreds and, who would have thought,
so much blood in her . . .
Not wanting to waste, I am here learning about the strain

through the fine mesh, the salt, the preparation of,
the preparation for an end that I can honor, can see
clearly enough might have been beginning.

Your body'd gone

silent. *Unresponsive* was the word
paraded around. I, crossing your arms,
felt my own muscles itching to uppercut—
to unsmug them right out of their lab coats.

You settled on another salvation:
site of stables, dust, sunlight, a wheelchair
of height and twitch. A horseshoe nailed
above the entrance, luck-side up.
My bones ached irony—Hope Corrals.
A valuable operation, under-funded.

We took you on a Tuesday afternoon
like this was beginning. No naïveté of morning.
None of Sunday's goodbye nonsense.

We, your reluctant attendants: sudden believers.
Shasta, and Tunstall Sue, and Westward
approached, bent their heads, soft mouths
to your quiet oat-filled hands. Westward
was everything as he brushed his mouth over your hair—
as no one moved to smooth—knowing
this gift of tangle and moist was more
than years of us crossing, uncrossing.

Ascent to Shasta's back—the certified
disabled saddle. Your beautiful, overmuch
helmet, and that slow gait of horse and rider.
A cycle punctuated with the tap of hardground hoof
and your *here now, here now,* encouragement
I'd swear was meant for all of us.

The River's Mouth

once:

We've always known. Death
unhinges the jaw.

Ptah, in his feathered costume
of a cast-out delta religion,
awash in a protestant nation's
exhibition hall. *Implements
to mouth,* a placard sedately
relates a calling out of spells to restore.

There was a limbering of the lips
with old world libations, *ritual, known
as The Opening of the Mouth.*

twice:

Sixteen and lost in Nebraska
in the ripening confusion "here dear
meet some of your kin, your
age." A family reunion
with cousins training
for death. The family biz
out Midwest, of dressing up the dead.

Morticians, the Latin rose
to the surface in that word.
A career fair a week before
beautician, mathematician, no
mention of this

the body's mouth was then
touched. The spells these young
men with my blood must know:
how to match the lips of the gone
with the memories
looking in: "Desert Rose, yes, her
favorite." open casket; closed

sarcophagus. Either way.

thrice:

A boat beneath.
A pair of wings.

Spells to restore the senses were recited.

Farmland and lace collars, bird
gods and gilt mummiform
statues. Requests across ages

for a final inspiration. Desire
held to the lips of those
who have no need.

Statistician . . .

Mead Memo Notebook Spiral, Yellow (II)

You loved Gainsborough, it seems.
Many notes on his life, a man of parts.
"Although he preferred landscape painting . . .
he set out to perfect his skills at portraiture."
So you've chosen the middle ground as homage,
both brazen individual and echo of the field.
You've sketched star thistle—that invasive—
with "yellow" printed on the page
and an arrow to the bloom that would be in time
and would be the color of the notebook cover:
a referential wormhole to this middle page
where the blue of the cheap ballpoint is
gobbling up and overtaking your fine lines.
An echo of the creature in the rendering.

The Yield

And the saints I don't fear
because they are long dead
become the rice fields
that impose
because they reflect outwards
and very much alive (to be dead)
just like saints; their death means
nothing unless we give it to them
too early; just like Christ; this rice
etching its exquisitely minute swears
bent in low and constant

and this is a blasphemy
but only blasphemy in an age that allows
the way the water in a rice field flows
toward harvest. Redemption begins with
a scythe, says saint, says Christ, says any grain,
prostrate wheat, penitent barley,
says bread broken together on our knees
on our knees. Says broken.

—

Four for a Grandmother and Her Past

1.

Cow, sheep, goat—
gleamtooth of miniature,
never that slough of dust. Shined,
this window-sill circus act,
like milking: every morning.

2.

You joke-shop your birth:
Pa and the ether-soaked rag
knocked your ma flat out
for days. *Been allergic ever since,*
you grin. Not looking up once.

3.

The nativity
is shaky in your slow hands:
Mary, Joseph, *She*
was too young to leave us . . .
You steady, move on to the star.

4.

Warm wheat: lofted sway.
Apron snug across your chest
you balance lemonades
and the eyes of six farmhands
who lean, lift brows, keep leaning,
spit just far enough.

Netsuke V: Octopus

The pupils of the octopus
are inlaid with horn.
They sound the sound
with collected light:
irises of trumpet,
antlers of the eye,
the synesthesia of
artifact embraced.
A vision-clutch beyond an old revered
multiplicity of arms.

One argument for maple and pine-lined over marble

statuary throwing *stay* out onto garden paths.
  Itself never getting between *begins* and *ends.* At *there.* At *least.*
   While the whole of living claims a way up as October begins,

wants an *enough.* Wants an *or:* an option to make crèches
  in which to rest the sick on brightly fallen leaves.
   The option to adopt the consequential stubbornness

of earthworms that never need to right themselves:
  the whole of living secure in *forward.* And the plea
   shall this pass too. Even old ouroboros eating

its own tail is a way up: if only to connect, make lovely
  through-lines, links like the fans on the cone to the tree
   that casts it out to cut the stays of death, to *between*

itself. Like the worm that through the valley of
  the eye of the needle will pass, through me,
   through The Kingdom of phylum, class, order, family . . .

The Fourth Dynasty in Limestone

Pepy is carved largest, as is customary.
Egyptian for the most important figure. Mother
to the two boys, or the one. It is not
our world, where one exists but once.

The boy at her knee,
the boy at her shoulder
may be all the child she ever knew.
It is not our world. One is set in stone
and then again. Perhaps we understand:

it is Picasso and moment after moment
on the turning face, on cube-planed face
all the movements of an eye in one fell swoop—
Time's uncustomary reconciliations.

How would we be, in our world, doubled
up in time around you? Mother
to the two girls,

and the one.

First Season's Monsoon

The trees are dropping their stores
of songbirds:
wet, cattywampus-footed
feather lumps.

Crippled with thick water.
Wings raised like curiously-weighted-with-what capes.
And eyes,
they are almost all eyes startling up.

Stooping to handcup a small, slick clump
I hunch and straighten
in one smooth, hesitant motion.
Rising without the maybe-it'll-drown.

Never touch a fallen bird.
Your smell will bring a peckdeath
from other birds: mama and papa birds.

I look up at the sound
of the breaking open or slamming shut.

Cheval de Frise and Gone-Sweetness at the All-Inclusive

Vacation with sand and they are parasols, paper parasols
in my drinks. Umbrellas are for keeping the rain
off and atop. Parasols of this size are for insinuating,
yet again, sun into the equation of relaxation
and open tabs. Tabs on beer are canned laughter here.
Here, nothing is contained in more secure a vault
than paper or plastic: consumer echoes can't be missed.
Neither can one miss the presence of the not-there beer bottle
in the hand worth two on the walls all around: broken bits
to keep one off the atop: embedded sharp and sun in green,
in amber (after rain, which never comes here but must) sans dust.
There has been a poem about this before. About this
severe accessory of height and trespass.
I tell you this is not news: this is a rebroadcast from the mind
spending its American time uncomfortably abroad in its own skin.
I tell you, despite this, there is no cover to be found.
Not even between another's covers. The parasol yields everything.

Cloud Vineyards

[Santorini, Greece]

high on hillsides and stone-low. windwhips.
[the grapes]

more wine than water out there.
[the mainlanders]

we live the illusion of snow. our towns like a powder atop.
[the islanders]

Thera, Atlantis, terroir of mists and long ago abrupt.
[the archeologists]

by the case and cherry tomatoes, caper berries.
[the tourists]

[the sea]

Phoenix

you are the soft spot in my heart for manifest destiny
and phrases like manifest destiny, like soft spot
for the complex desires of Michelin-starred restaurants in strip
    malls.
you remind me of the ghost town that as a child we would visit
just for the day because no water, expansion too quick,
    conditions too harsh.
you remind me in your earnest art and moneyed cocktail
    lounges of everything
denied. the boy glittering on the stage,
lip-syncing along no sound not having the guts to confront
what epicenter is. what sometimes doesn't rise, doesn't ash, but
    burns and burns.

Early Artichokes

Flowers of green shale, opening,
and opening scales spreading.

Who stops up an ear
for not hearing? Death is less
than wicked point leaves. There is a listening
in the sun: a forgiving we won't touch
that they will.

The artichokes
are living up and out. Most times they don't hear
anything but half haystacks
coming into a new brilliance.

Tasting Notes for Two Liquid (de)Vices

1.

Mauve loft. Bell-drags: Tokay mush and thirst,
blush-virus, thin necessity from seed.

It's undertow: come rib-eye alarms, slight capers!
We bear Flames, and grigios: quiet flights.

2.

Merry peat: nose assault. Iamb: ∪ /
Pith and clot or wishpan: a briny sport.

3.

Errata:

Implied wine, whisky. Read: life,
death (celebrations pertaining to).

Any order.

Netsuke III: Snake

What's taken from you is possibility.
Your approach, the whisper at my ear,
the thrill of the chase, the knowledge
you could malice me with movement:
shed your skin with a toss of your head,
a twist where my hips would be.

Shiny Magazine on the Finer Things

I. What Chefs Want to Know about Time (Wine)

The DMV line is a reduction,
aromatic and simmering compact
to flavor the kiosk's open mouth.
Fake-tan—carrot skins; meth-father—
onions, roast bones weeping
marrow through concentric rings, saw marks.

How did we get here: "smile—no teeth"
chin up is not parallel parking and we all fear the kale
of the freeway merge. Crisp sound of fender to paint,
fork to gristle. "Lovely, work for the cinema."
Those stories cling to the palate without tannins.

The employee's hand, thin
slender, is shaped for pushing
garlic under chicken skin, for reaching
between alternator and manifold
to finger-pinch the dropped spatula.

II. Travel: New Orleans on Six Meals a Day

No mascara on once meant a bad day.
I heard "everybody's got a dead-guy story,
now." The crab shacks are closed—the
debutant diners don't know where the line ends,
how to make dirty rice with that taste
caught in every single orifice.

They say the flavors of a Po' Boy
should run from the elbows,
color the floor, the thighs of your jeans.
Everyone has their story, no
one asks about water stained ceilings.

Everybody wants to stain their thighs
at least once in their life. With God
or man—everyone wants to
to snap the back of the crawfish—suck
out the head for flavor. Salvage.

Fourteen Minutes Too Late for the Cheese Counter

And though I've loved many, each in their turn, the fact of a man is not the same as a really good Camembert and never will be. These are the riddles of pleasure: that it won't always overtake fact, but often does. I left him out to sit for three or four days. At room temperature. You've got to wait until you know it is there across the room, the Camembert. So says Dmitri—French—so he should know. It's so Sondheim or Hammerstein: *across a crowded room* you would know, just know somehow. Aged in his cave. Ready to drag you around the room by your tongue, swinging that triumphant culinary club and stinking to high heaven. But the lock is turned on that night. And I'd honestly take an American Single at this point, square little bland dazzlers all lined up to be paired with whatever is on offer. Melt to me, Manhattan! Treat me like I'm all the quality this block's got, like I'm something to pour into a flute: Champagne or pitch me in the key of C. Tonight each breath is stretching its chilled self like a canvas before me. Fact catches up. I am sure Dali's watches wouldn't even run.

Roles and Reckoning near Solstice

In gender studies
(a fuzzy study unlike
optometry but no less vital
to vision), we discuss a continuum.
It is suggested that like
dusk   the boundaries aren't
discrete

. . .

Outside of Eskilstuna, Sweden:
there was twilight,
a disagreement between us,
and the fox in the field.

The way if you looked at the sky your eyes would flip one way/
rods or cones
if you looked at the field another\
(by you, I mean anyone, though you were there)
dark to light/
\light to dark.

It is where you think the longest night may take you:
the sky or the field.

The fox pouncing—beautiful arc of a body
at the death of something
that could not be seen.

. . .

That unmapped arc in the falling or rising night was triumph of
    trajectory,
was enough to   readjust us to the task.

If the fox was male\
was female/   I do know it claimed life.

. . .

You looked in my eyes, or I in

—

"Grand Rapids Arch"

Andy Goldsworthy, Meijer Gardens

I stood beneath this pressure that holds itself together by internal
   torque.

We were having a disagreement about something wildly intimate
and I had walked this cold clear path through the sculpture park
   on my own.
Its sedate Rodin and that Henry Moore: the one that thrusts a
   hip in bronze,
one what might have been
a hip or the bow of a back, in bronze, at me.

The blocks were scored with the lines of the pneumatic drills.
Like the impressions left
when a pair of fishnet stockings that's been caught slightly too
   tight on the plumb
of the calf are removed—echoes of where one's been:

imprints made on the body like tooth rivets on taste buds.
I can reach for you without knowing why,
the dentist's tool hard at it again
and my thick tongue lunging toward it.

I arrived and stood shaded in what I did not know was not
   secure,
might have thought twice that it would fall, but I did not and it
   didn't and I returned
south to you and the conversation that would push our
words against each other and up to form something vaulted:

a space created like our own bower, an arched gate hung with
   ribbons,
like rice lofting then
falling through the air, the bridge of my body, a rainbow later
   that day
almost too much—how it contains that supplication—that
   promise
held flush against the sky like screwing against a wall.
Slipping color down a sheering drop.

The Complex of the Yolk Base

I.

What brilliancy it must have been
at the get-go. The masterpiece
easy, Ptolemaic, at the bottom of the pestle:
pulse pleasure of yellow under the palette knife.

Everything pure seems mildly lurid lately.
The virginal is a bridge in Ohio if that's
what you're thinking.

Neil Diamond singing "Cherry, Cherry."

Lapis came in, ochre. The yolk would go bad
if you gave it enough time, or whisky.

II.

Bears eat the brains first. Only the brains
until the season demands salmon
devoured tail fin to topknot.

III.

I've begun to notice the infidelities
of drainage ditches at dusk.
Twilight allows an offshoot.

IV.

Horemheb offers wine to Anubis,
a sacred moment with
both wrists on sideways.

Netsuke II: [   ]

The one that as yet is not.
(un) Imaginably small detail:
wound as with the others,
clasped as like the others,
embryonic—I intuit—in symbol.
And yet, like a zygote of Byzantium
I tremble at what might . . .
I do so love the *oni*.
Love what sublime can spring from small things.

To Older Cold

Snow falls faster in the past.

Take that last great extinction:
our globe a soft-boiled egg—
the speed of its shell cracking.
It's the feel of tweed
spun from its loom just before the joints freeze.

Trapped in celluloid—projected—the fall hardly registers
before the splice, camera pan
to right, to the war, the kiss, the action.

Snow covers half my childhood.
It arrived in haste. It sank school days
on battery-operated radios,
storm shadows huddled electricity,
and windowsills succumbed often, and at speed.

Fresh fallen is too much, too likely,
for our slow aperture.

The Myrtle-Wood Bowl

Sweet meat of the clam is implied by tartar sauce.
In a drawing room that never dreamed of a stove,
much less a river, a bowl holds the bowls
of a dozen pulled-green clamshell alluvials:
freshwater and codependent by form, perhaps by nature.
The grain of this wood
is enough to flow any ebb a bottle of good Barolo might provide,
its revolution of underfoot on the tongue.

This underfoot requires a streambed or forest,
depending on what regret we are modifying.
What is missing is often the Coos Bay, Oregon, of your great
    aunt, Colleen,
the Walnut grove of your grandfather,
before the triple bypass, before the blight.

And there is the rub, which it is understood you need
before the roast. If this bowl bellowed walnut
it would be sanctuary by form alone.
Its beating heart saved by sitting on the shelf. A ruin of a tree
is all the future our century can hold.
The bypass would have uncored it anyway.
A grave good of so rare a whatnot. A one-off.
And our own beat immortality in our clamshell chests,
our ribs wandering the decades before they'll unclasp:
opening like brackish water to the sea.

Why Would Anyone Want to Live[1]
(Couplets for a Hero)

February 2011

On the horizon: a dead god's new book.[2]
The interviews are breathtaking. Edgy.[3]

Dog races come inexplicably[4]
to mind. Sweet numbered cloaks all bolting West.[5]

A metaphor of muscle, circling, strain,[6]
onward toward the rabbit hole in broad sun.[7]

I hear they put them down. No Wonderland[8]
awaits. Except, perhaps in footnotes. Please,[9]

tell me more about the shore, O Pale King![10]
from your Midwestern tennis court, hold sway.[11]

---

1 The complete quote from David Foster Wallace is on media
   saturation: "Why would anyone want to live when they could watch."
2 The radio is bristling: "First Look!"
3 Still, a slather of guilt, of over-dredging.
4 (Although some might see capability.)
5 Or shocking East, but straight toward some sure bet.
6 The geometry of loop, trap, of pain.
7 Everyone looked, gasped at what was gone (done).
8 A world writ by his hand. By his own hand.
9 Awake! Accept some facts (in footnotes = pleas).
10 The egrets pixilated: photo things.
11 I've seen the sea ten thousand times, you say.

Barcelona

Which your grandfather calls Barcalounger
every single time. And it does get funnier.

—

We've heard the tour guides say it more than once:
how the cathedral architect's picture postcards got wet—
dripping buttresses onto our third dimension
from flat plans to go-go cathedral gravy.

I've wanted it to be so:
the triumph of vision in the corruption of.
A comfort there.

—

On the napkin with which I was going to wipe my mouth
you've drawn another swordfish in a circle of stars
that is actually a sailfish.

—

It's been long years now I have been doubting
how the phrase goes. The details: either
God's there or the Devil's in them.

Vanguard Aria for Minor Organs

A shriek in the system of what might have been: an
avant-garde—a collective now and future.
By definition, an elaborate song for solitary voice.

How it goes when the line steps back
a choir of combatants, brothers in arms
all in the same breath.

You out there on the front, wailing. Stage lights up
on the black sheep.

Foremost of everything to never come.
An appendicitis of the spirit. Prepare to be bullied
by the rude health of divergence.

In response to *cut it out:*
"I wasn't even touching you."
Touch or be cut.

In art, in tonsillectomies,
if it doesn't catch in the throat, then.

Evolutionary fingers to the wrist taking inventory,
innovation become a falling song of impulse.

Reassurance in Negative Space

... to being oneself, a wedge-shaped core of darkness, something invisible to others.
—Virginia Woolf

Sounds like something Keats would say
about something that wasn't there.

When Pound wrote "photography" in Eliot's margin did he mean
the print, or the negative, or the print?

You talk about Berryman anecdotally and I never answer.
But, no, I don't think *wickedness is soluble in art.*

Herbert's angel is on its side on Easter in a lot of editions.
Centerfold angel. But try not to hum that tune: resurrection should be
    selective.

Poems of childbirth are just over my head, one says earnestly.
That is not where they are.

Tell someone you believe in the Roman road and they'll try to swerve you
    off religion
to metaphor: *It's there. In the middle of everything.*

The triangular iceberg in the steak house, amidst the blue cheese, not
    afloat,
has Hemingway all wrong.

He said something to the titanic subconscious in fractional terms,
but his cats' toes are at six-fifths so who can reckon.

I can say I love you here without fear of reprisals.
Which is a wicked thing to do.

There are just two fears:
that someone will come for you in the night. Or no one.

A Poem with Three Lines from One Night in Portland

While others of fine wine claimed to be experts
I convinced them all I had invented air, climbing through a window
in the center of the room that no one knew was there,
as no one sees the mime holding the banana until it is peeled.
Who tripped the wires, the wires every one!
The cry went out from widening eyes, lubricated uvulas,
as I emerged into the future an acrobatic witness.
And the fireplace warped the light, Debussy on low
caused boredom in perfectly lively jute rugs,
plants filled with spiders, glassware brimmed olive on olive on stick.
Someone was late or not coming after all,
politics began lolling a tongue over an end table.
And the merriment erupted at midnight into dark,
small doses of something that raised voices, required salt,
banging at doors and smashing windows
some didn't even know were there to be broken.

Night Being the Consort of Chaos in Milton

I. Slippage

How cliché and wonderful soap bubbles in moonlight in
slight wind in descent and alternating ascent with
meteoric qualities that outstrip ephemera. Bel cantos to any any.

The word *diadem* an ornament to tongue if not to crown.
The crown: a chakra all up and out (but of in) and rainbow rise.
Breath fills the bubbles—the breath the air has been becomes
     becoming.

The profane and sacred are both Molotov cocktails, aren't they,
waiting to be lit by the opposing side and lobbed back at us?
At least that's what the canopy thought and the canapé too.
One covered needlessly in chives and sour cream, the other—
     quite needfully.

II. Gentleness

And I can *bon vivant* as well as the next.

Roundabout the night with tight attenuations, articulations of
     splendor

manifested in angular libations that lead onward into the spilt-light
     estate of crowd.

However, you, my dear, are of salmon cooked long until it is falling
     flesh and salt and plain black pepper

and humble mayonnaise that mimics that slow fat of the fish that
     allows the grill to make

of this day a scent and ruddy pink wonder and leaves to memory
     alone the desire for

spicy stacked tapas that hint night & vexing intrusive escalation.

These hours, now, consist of lament at star thistle's encroachment—
     speaking of land and its tethers—

at the Delta's penchant for sandbars this season, at the gravity of
     saying anything at ten a.m.

III. *felix culpa*

Through the palpable obscure, Muse, urge onward.

Kick the luminary lunch bags to flame on holidays,
and drop avocados into the channels of Mars.

Fell the shrines each diner makes of the condiments.
O melting arctic and savage modus operandi!

Salt them with sweat from a dance with a name,
those pistachios I eat at roasted dusk.

Copulate near a bicycle and throw oblivious
peaches at catfish that swim near enough.

Sundown is a thing both locked and
and, Muse, don't you know it. Fall already, beautiful.

—

Notes

Barcelona owes a nod to Larry Levis's "Elegy with a Bridle in Its Hand."

Cakes and Ale's Snyder is Gary Snyder whose pages are radiant, if often beautifully broken things. The quote in the poem is from W. Somerset Maugham's novel of that title, which itself is taken from Shakespeare's "Twelfth Night": "Dost thou think, because thou art virtuous, there shall be no more cakes and ale?" (2.3.).

a call for catechresis is indebted to commentary by abstract painter Tess Jaray.

Cellar Physic is an obscure euphemism for medicine from the cellar, such as wine. Those self-medicating do not always stick to the recommended dosage.

Cheval de Frise and Gone-Sweetness at the All-Inclusive references Carolyn Forché's "The Colonel" wherein broken bottles are embedded in security walls to deter intruders.

Inventory from a One-Hour Room contains a line from H.D.'s roman à clef *The Sword Went out to Sea.*

On Looking Again into Wright's *Forklift, Ohio* is indebted to *Outtakes* (Sarabande) that reproduces Charles Wright's original typescripts from *Forklift, Ohio.*

Netsuke I: Crab: Netsuke are small toggles carved from ivory, wood, etc., and were used to attach a purse to a belt in traditional Japanese dress— now commonly viewed as collector/ornamental items.

Netsuke IV: Ashinaga & Tenaga: Ashinaga and Tenaga are characterized by long arms and long legs.

Night Being the Consort of Chaos in Milton: final section's italics from John Milton's *Paradise Lost* (2. 404). The title refers to that epic's allegorical figures.

A Poem with Three Lines from one Night in Portland includes three lines from "One Night in Portland" from Deborah Digges's *The Wind Blows Through the Doors of My Heart*.

Preparing Trout Caviar in the First Trimester contains a paraphrase from Shakespeare's *Macbeth*.

Reading Ostriker and Archeology Today for Spiritual Guidance: italics from Alicia Ostriker's "Matisse, Too."

Reassurance in Negative Space's epigraph is from Woolf's *To the Lighthouse*. Ernest Hemingway's famous theory of omission has it that "The dignity of movement of an ice-berg is due to only one-eighth of it being above water. A writer who omits things because he does not know them only makes hollow places in his writing." The descendants of his polydactyl cats are still a source of curiosity at The Hemingway House in Key West, Florida.

Or What You Will owes its title to Shakespeare and his play "Twelfth Night; or, What You Will" in which the twins Viola and Sebastian are looked at by many. It also is indebted to the verve of Matthew Dickman's *Mayakovski's Revolver*. It may, in some way, also be indebted to his twin brother.

Why Would Anyone Want to Live (Couplets for a Hero): a set of heroic couplets, is indebted to the BBC Radio 3 Sunday Feature: "Endnotes: David Foster Wallace."

—

Elizabyth A. Hiscox is the author of *Inventory from a One-Hour Room.* She served as Poet-in-Residence at Durham University (UK) and is recipient of Arizona Commission on the Arts and Vermont Studio Center Grants. Also selected for the Seventh Avenue Streetscape public-art initiative, her poetry was displayed on a central-Phoenix billboard for a year in conjunction with the city's First Friday art walks. Hiscox holds an MFA from Arizona State University and a PhD from Western Michigan University in Kalamazoo. She has taught writing in England, the Czech Republic, and Spain and currently instructs at Western State Colorado University where she is founding director of the Contemporary Writer Series.

ALSO FROM WORD GALAXY PRESS

Margaret Rockwell Finch, *Crone's Wines: Late Poems*

Emily Grosholz, *The Stars of Earth: New and Selected Poems*

A.G. Harmon, *Some Bore Gifts – Stories*

www.wordgalaxy.com

ood-product-compliance

053

1 9 2 7 4 0 9 9 8 5 *